KINU

Korea Institute for National Unification

Energy Cooperation with North Korea: Issues and Suggestions

Kyuryoon Kim

The Korea Institute for National Unification (KINU) is a non-profit government research organization commissioned to study issues regarding peace settlement on the Korean Peninsula and the unification of the two Koreas. It is contributing to the reconciliation and cooperation of the two Koreas as well as their unification through basic research on related affairs, the development of a policy on national unification, and the formation of a national consensus.

ISBN No.: 89-8479-328-0-93340   ₩ 4,500

Published 2005 by KINU

535-353 Suyu 6-dong, Gangbuk-gu, Seoul 142-887, South Korea
www.kinu.or.kr
To order KINU documents or to obtain additional information, contact Distribution Services: Telephone 82-2-901-2559/2520, or the Government Publication Sales Center 82-2-734-6818.

Energy Cooperation with North Korea: Issues and Suggestions / Kyuryoon Kim – Seoul: the Korea Institute for National Unification, 2005

p. ; cm. – (Studies series ; 05-04)

ISBN 89-8479-328-0-93340

322.8311-KDC4
337.5193-DDC21   CIP2005002859

Energy Cooperation with North Korea:
Issues and Suggestions

About the Author

Kyuryoon Kim is a Senior Research Fellow at the Korea Institute for National Unification. He received his PhD from Northwestern University in 1989, MA from Northwestern University, and BA from Sogang University, Seoul, Korea. His research interests include international political economy, Asia-Pacific cooperation, and Korean unification studies. He is the author of numerous articles including recently published "Regional Cooperation in East Asia" and "International Political Economy of Energy Cooperation in Northeast Asia" in 2005.

*   *   *

Energy Cooperation with North Korea: Issues and Suggestions

Contents

Contents

Contents

Tables

Figures

Chapter One

Introduction

The North Korean economy has been in a great depression because of its mismanagement and inefficiency in dealing with the repercussions from the collapse of the socialist bloc. North Korea has been suffering from shortages in three sectors: food, foreign exchange, and energy. The instability in supplying energy for industry has in particular hampered its economic recovery. Energy is indispensable in achieving economic development because energy supply plays an important role in supporting the smooth flow of industrial activities. North Korea needs to have a systematic plan to develop its energy sector in order to provide adequate levels of energy supply. Indeed, it is necessary for North Korea to solve its energy shortage problems to recover from its economic downturns. It is also necessary for North Korea to have external relations in order to provide its industries with petroleum. It is unthinkable to attempt economic development with an isolated economic policy within the highly interdependent world economy. While the North Korean energy problem was initially caused by the collapse of the socialist bloc, it was aggravated because North Korea did not pursue economic exchanges with capitalist countries during the 1990s and onward.

North Korea maintained its policy of self-reliance in the energy sector as it did with other sectors of the economy. As a result, energy efficiency has dropped significantly and resulted in lower productivity within the industry. Recently, coal production has declined and has caused a near collapse of the energy supply system because of North Korea's heavy reliance on coal to supply energy to its industries. This phenomenon has been aggravated by the reduction of the energy supply from the former socialist allies, namely China and Russia.

In order to solve North Korean energy problems, North Korea needs to open up its economy and adopt market mechanisms. Indeed, it recently changed some economic measures to include market mechanisms in its management of the national economy. However, North Korea still maintains socialist and self-reliance policies. North Korea's recent economic policy changes have been reactive rather than proactive because of the continuous concern from its leadership about the possible adverse impacts of opening up the economy. As a result, it is hard to imagine a complete recovery of energy shortages in the short run. Thus, it is necessary for us to devise a plan to solve the North Korean energy problems in a more systematic way based on longer term perspectives. The current research is an attempt to provide a plan to reduce the North Korean energy problems. The first section deals with the current condition of the North Korean energy sector. The second section is devoted to identifying the causes behind the North Korean energy problems. The third section attempts to provide cooperative schemes for possible solutions.

Chapter Two

Current Conditions of the North Korean

Energy Industry

To analyze current conditions of the North Korean energy industry, this section shall deal with the North Korean energy policy. Since North Korea maintains a socialist regime in the running of its economy, an investigation of governmental policy concerning energy is important in order to understand causes behind the current difficulties. Then an explanation about the overall production and consumption structure, based on the past fifteen years of energy data, shall be provided. In doing so, the comparison between South and North Korea shall be delineated in order to draw implications for possible areas of cooperation.

North Korean Energy Policy

North Korea has maintained a self-reliant, central command economy since its foundation. A self-reliant economy typically aims for internal self-sufficiency, while neglecting economic exchanges with the outside world. The North Korean energy sector also follows the principle of self-reliance. North Korea has devoted most of its efforts to the maximization of the domestic production of coal. As a result, the North Korean energy policy lacks in economic efficiency and productivity. At the same time, North Korea limits the import of energy to the types it cannot produce domestically.

North Korea is abundantly endowed with coal. It has emphasized the development of mining and processing coal. However, the North Korean energy industry has never been self-reliant because it lacks oil and cokes. Consequently, the North Korean energy policy has focused on minimizing the use of oil and cokes.[1]

North Korea has emphasized the importance of self-reliance as follows.[2] They state that it is necessary for them to build a domestic primary product industry and a fuel-producing industry in order to achieve a self-reliant national economy. They also state that it is necessary to have domestic raw materials and fuel foundations in order to be a stable and developing economy.

The North Korean energy industry can be divided into three categories: raw material production to support mining and electricity production, coal and mineral production to support fuel consumption, and electricity production as a power source. North Korea has continuously emphasized the importance of self-reliance in order to achieve a successful Juche industry by supplying the peoples' economy with domestically produced raw materials, fuel, and power sources. It also prioritizes the domestic production of energy

---

[1] Woojin Jung, "Comparison between South and North Korean Energy Systems," *Petroleum Association Magazine* (1993), p. 115 (In Korean).
[2] Youngrong Chung, "The Utilization of Factor Endowment," *Economy Research*, Vol. 2 (2001), pp. 29~31 (In Korean).

over the scientifically advanced production lines and industrial structures. In other words, North Korea believes the industries with imported energy sources should be replaced by the ones with domestically produced energy.[3]

Utilizing this economic strategy, North Korea emphasizes the development of its mining industry and the construction of hydro-electric power plants. Subsequently, North Korea has made a great effort at domestically producing anthracite (smokeless) coal. However, production of smokeless coal has been on the decline since 1990. North Korea has imported oil from China and Russia, but these countries have decreased exports of oil to North Korea since the early 1990s. At the same time, they have also cancelled friendly price mechanisms which have been applied to the energy trade. All of these factors can be attributed to the chronic shortage situation of the North Korean energy sector.

In the 1990s, North Korea made an effort in promoting alternative energy development, such as small scale hydroelectric power generation and wind power plant projects, in order to compensate for the low production of coal and the decreasing generation of hydro-electric power. These efforts have largely failed because North Korea could not mobilize the necessary investment to promote the development of alternative energy sources. As a matter of fact, alternative energy development projects are carried out in advanced countries for the purpose of solving environmental problems, which originate from excessive fossil fuel consumption. Thus, alternative energy development projects, which generally have an environmental focus, cannot be successful in countries like North

---

[3] Woojin Jung, *North Korean Energy Industry* (Seoul: Korean Overseas Information Service, 1996), p. 14 (In Korean).

Korea because their primary aim is not to increase the supply of energy.

North Korea has been able to maintain low levels of dependence on foreign energy sources in spite of its scarce energy endowment, except for coal and hydroelectric power, because it has maintained closed economic policies. Recently, North Korea has again emphasized the importance of coal and hydroelectricity production in order to build the economy during the military first era. According to Kim Jong-Il, it is necessary to solve electric shortage problems first and advance the coal and railroad industries. It was also pointed out that in order to carry out the military production plan, it is necessary to guarantee electricity and coal.[4]

The North Korean Energy Industry

As noted above, North Korea relies heavily on coal and hydroelectric power as its primary source of energy. It is hard to figure out accurate amounts of energy consumption because of the closed character of North Korea's economic management. As a matter of fact, several institutions such as the International Energy Agency (IEA), the United Nations (UN), and the Ministry of Unification (MOU) provide us with energy related statistics. Analysts have always questioned the validity of this data. In order to provide a macro perspective on North Korea's energy supply and demand, let us begin with the basic economic indicators of North Korean economy.

North Korea recorded continuous negative economic growth rates

---

4 Dukho Kim, "Necessary Requirements of Military First Era," *Economy Research*, Vol. 2 (2004), pp. 5~7 (In Korean).

during the 1990s as shown in <Table II-1>. As a result, the figure for the 1998 Gross National Income (GNI) is only 54.5% of the 1990 GNI, which means the North Korean economy shrunk by about half during the 1990s. As North Korea began to show positive economic growth beginning in 1999, the GNI of 2004 showed 20.4 billion dollars, which was still lower than the 1990 figure. When we compare the North Korean economy with South Korea, we can note that North Korean GNI of 1990 was only 8.8% of the South Korean GNI. This gap widened in 2004 as the table below shows. The South Korean GNI became 32.8 times that of the North

<Table Ⅱ-1> Economic Growth Rates: North and South Korea

	North Korea			South Korea				
	GNI (Billion Dollars), (A)	Growth Rate (%)	GNI Per Capita (Dollar), (a)	GNI (Billion Dollars), (B)	Growth Rate (%)	GNI Per Capita (Dollar), (b)	(B)/(A)	(b)/(a)
1990	23.1	-3.7	1142	263.5	9.2	6,147	11.4	5.4
1991	22.9	-3.5	1115	307.6	9.4	7,105	13.5	6.4
1992	21.1	-6	1013	329.3	5.9	7,527	15.6	7.4
1993	20.5	-4.2	969	361.4	6.1	8,177	17.7	8.4
1994	21.2	-2.1	992	422.3	8.5	9,459	19.9	9.5
1995	22.3	-4.1	1034	515.5	9.2	11,432	23.1	11.1
1996	21.4	-3.6	989	555.3	7	12,197	25.9	12.3
1997	17.7	-6.3	811	513.6	4.7	11,176	29.1	13.8
1998	12.6	-1.1	573	340.4	-6.9	7,355	27.1	12.8
1999	15.8	6.2	714	440.0	9.5	9,438	27.9	13.2
2000	16.8	1.3	757	509.6	8.5	10,841	30.4	14.3
2001	15.7	3.7	706	481.1	3.8	10,162	30.6	14.4
2002	17.0	1.2	762	547.5	7	11,493	32.1	15.1
2003	18.4	1.8	818	608.6	3.1	12,720	33.1	15.6
2004	20.8	2.2	914	681.0	4.6	14,162	32.8	15.5

Source: The Bank of Korea <http://www.bok.or.kr/template/main/html/index.jsp?tbl=tbl_FM 0000000066_CA0000000701>.

Korean GNI. When we look at the GNI per capita figures, the South Korean GNI per capita of 2004 was 15.5 times of the North Korean GNI per capita.

As shown in <Table II-2>, North Korea's energy supply amount in 1990 was 2.4 million Tons of Oil Equivalent (TOE), and it decreased to 1.4 million TOE in 1998. Starting in 1999, North Korea began to show signs of a small economic recovery and by 2003, it recorded 1.6 million TOE. North Korea's economy had already showed major problems in 1990, and since energy supply in 2003 was only about 2/3 of the 1990 level, it is evident that the economy was still facing major difficulties. When we consider the recovery of the overall

<Table II-2> Energy Uses of North and South Korea

	Energy Consumption (Thousand TOE)			Energy Consumption Per Capita (TOE)		
	North (A)*	South (B)**	(B)/(A)	North (a)	South (b)	(b)/(a)
1990	23,963	93,192	3.9	1.19	2.17	1.80
1991	21,920	103,619	4.7	1.07	2.39	2.20
1992	20,450	116,010	5.7	0.98	2.65	2.70
1993	19,013	126,879	6.7	0.90	2.87	3.20
1994	17,870	137,234	7.7	0.84	3.07	3.70
1995	17,280	150,437	8.7	0.80	3.34	4.20
1996	15,836	165,212	10.4	0.73	3.63	5.00
1997	14,746	180,638	12.2	0.68	3.93	5.80
1998	14,030	165,932	11.8	0.64	3.58	5.60
1999	14,955	181,363	12.1	0.68	3.89	5.70
2000	15,687	192,887	12.3	0.71	4.10	5.80
2001	16,230	198,409	12.2	0.73	4.19	5.70
2002	15,638	208,636	13.3	0.70	4.38	6.30
2003	16,079	215,067	13.4	0.71	4.49	6.30

Source: Korea National Statistical Office, *Comparison of South and North Korean Socio-Economic Data* (Seoul: Korea National Statistical Office, 2004), p. 81.
*Supply Amount; **Consumption Amount.

economy, as we discussed in the previous table, North Korea recovered from the record low of 1998 to 80% of the 1990 record high in 2003. However, energy supply was only 67% of the 1990 level in 2003. This signifies that North Korea's energy problem had been much more severe than other sectors of the economy. In comparison, South Korean energy use was 3.9 times greater than that of North Korea. In 2003, this gap widened further as South Korean energy use was 13.4 times greater than that of North Korea. To further analyze these statistics, we can compare records of GNI with energy use. The GNI gap between South and North Korea is even greater than the energy use gap. This reflects the inefficiency of North Korea's energy use. In other words, South Korea had advanced into a developed country model in using energy, while North Korea had wasted its energy because of mismanagement.

By examining the composition of North Korean energy supply in <Table II-3>, we can see that coal was by far the largest source of energy. Between 1990 and 2003, coal accounted for about 70% of the total energy consumption in North Korea. The second most important source of North Korean energy was hydroelectric power, accounting for 15.7% of total energy consumption in 1990 and 18.2% in 2003. The third most important energy source was oil. In fact, oil provided 10.5% of the energy supply in 1990 and dropped significantly to 5.1% in 1994. Then it recovered from its low point to approximately 7-8% in the 2000s. This heavy dependence on coal and hydroelectric power caused North Korea to continuously concentrate its efforts on developing coal mines and hydroelectric power plants. In contrast, the South Korean energy mix structure was distributed relatively evenly among the sources: oil at about 50%, coal at about 20%, and nuclear energy at about 10-15%. However, South Korea imports almost all of its energy from overseas.

<Table Ⅱ-3> Energy Mix of North and South Korea

(Unit: Thousand TOE, %)

			1990	1991	1992	1993	1994	1995	1996
North Korea*		Total	23,963	21,920	20,450	19,013	17,870	17,280	15,836
	Rate	Coal	69.2	70.7	71.4	71.3	71.1	68.6	66.3
		Oil	10.5	8.6	7.4	7.2	5.1	6.4	9.1
		Hydro	15.7	17.1	17.4	17.4	19.4	20.5	19.6
		Nuclear	0.0	0.0	0.0	0.0	0.0	0.0	0.0
		LNG	0.0	0.0	0.0	0.0	0.0	0.0	0.0
		MISC	4.7	3.6	3.8	4.2	4.4	4.6	5.0
South Korea**		Total	93,192	103,619	116,010	126,879	137,234	150,437	165,212
	Ratio	Coal	26.2	23.7	20.4	20.4	19.4	18.7	19.5
		Oil	53.8	57.5	61.8	61.9	62.9	62.5	60.5
		Hydro	1.7	1.2	1.0	1.2	0.7	0.9	0.8
		Nuclear	14.2	13.6	12.2	11.5	10.7	11.1	11.2
		LNG	3.2	3.4	3.9	4.5	5.6	6.1	7.4
		MISC	0.9	0.6	0.6	0.5	0.7	0.7	0.7
			1997	1998	1999	2000	2001	2002	2003
North Korea		Total	14,746	14,030	14,955	15,687	16,230	15,640	16,079
	Ratio	Coal	69.8	66.3	70.2	71.7	71.2	70.0	69.3
		Oil	6.8	10.0	5.9	7.1	7.7	8.0	7.6
		Hydro	18.0	18.2	18.7	16.2	16.3	17.0	18.2
		Nuclear	0.0	0.0	0.0	0.0	0.0	0.0	0.0
		LNG	0.0	0.0	0.0	0.0	0.0	0.0	0.0
		MISC	5.3	5.5	5.2	5.0	4.8	5.0	4.9
South Korea		Total	180,638	165,932	181,363	192,887	198,409	208,636	215,067
	Ratio	Coal	19.3	21.7	21.0	22.2	23.0	23.5	23.8
		Oil	60.4	54.6	53.6	52.1	50.7	49.1	47.6
		Hydro	0.7	0.9	0.9	0.7	0.5	0.6	0.8
		Nuclear	10.7	13.5	14.2	14.1	14.1	14.3	15.1
		LNG	8.2	8.4	9.3	9.8	10.5	11.1	11.2
		MISC	0.7	0.9	1.0	1.1	1.2	1.4	1.5

Source: Korea National Statistical Office, *Comparison of South and North Korean Socio-Economic Data*, p. 82~83.
*Supply Amount; **Consumption Amount.

Chapter Three

Sectoral Situations of the North Korean

Energy Industry

North Korea has long been dependent on coal as a major source of energy. Policies surrounding coal production and consumption shall be provided in order to understand the reasons behind the overdependence on coal by the North Korean government. It shall be followed by an investigation of the production potentials and the actual supply levels for the past decade. The second most important source of energy in North Korea is electricity. In order to draw implications for the possible cooperation areas, this section shall provide comparisons between South and North Korea regarding electricity generation. Then the past history of nuclear energy development shall be discussed briefly. Indeed, North Korea's nuclear development activities received much attention from the international community because of its possible dual usages. The following section will deal with such issues in more detail.

Coal Industry

Coal Policy

In North Korea, coal plays an important role in supporting the Juche industry. Thus enhancement of oil production has been prioritized to develop the peoples' economy. It is necessary to maximize production of coal at the mine site first to guarantee the normal development of subsequent processing industries. All these efforts should result in a planned and balanced development of the peoples' economy.

North Korea adopted three policy guidelines to increase the productivity of coal production: securing domestic sources, enhancing mining efficiency, and developing processing technology. In order to achieve these policy objectives, North Korea set three principles for mining development: broadening geological exploration projects, realizing technological innovations, and actualizing scientific research projects.

First, geological exploration aims at securing more coal reserves. In order to achieve this goal, North Korea wants to modernize exploration equipment and reinforce manpower.

Second, technological innovations are related to modernization projects for efficient mining. More specifically, North Korea wants to mechanize coal mining work, drilling, blasting, digging, and transporting in order to systematically enhance mining capacity for coal.

Third, scientific research projects aim at developing practical techniques and improving management systems. It asks for enlargement of research facilities and reinforcement of research staff.

One of the peculiar characteristics in the North Korean coal policy can be noted as follows. On the one hand, high calorie coals are used for industrial purposes and exports. On the other hand, low calorie coals are used for household consumption. This dual policy stems from the worsening foreign currency situation and the policy of prioritizing heavy industry. As a result, coals for household heating are low calorie coals generally under 3,000 kcal/kg.

Coal Reserves
North Korean geological conditions allow for abundant sources of minerals such as graphite, zinc, magnesite, gold, silver, tungsten, molybdenum, and mica. Coal is deposited throughout the country. About 3/4 of the coal is deposited in South Pyungan Province. Lignites (brown coals) are deposited in North Hamgyung Province.[5]

In North Korea, anthracite coal is deposited in Pyungan Province and bituminous coal is deposited in Hamgung Province. Specifically, anthracite coals are from mines such as Samsin, Sadong, Yongsung, Heukryeong, Gangdong, Gangseo, Seongcheon, and Oncheon. The average width of North Korean coal mines is 3.9 meters and the maximum depth is 250 meters. Bituminous coal is deposited in mines such as Aoji, Obong, Eunsung, Gilgun, Hamyun, and Hyoryong.

Major coal mines are managed by the central government authorities in North Korea. About 100 coal mines are under the supervision of the central government. Provincial government authorities control

---

5 Kiyol Bang, *South and North Korean Energy Demand and Supply* (Gyonggido: Korea Energy Economics Institute, 1999), pp. 83~84 (In Korean).

around 500 small and medium size coal mines.

North Korean coal reserves are estimated to be 14.7 billion tons by the Korean Ministry of Unification. United Nations estimated 2.6 billion tons based on the confirmed reserves. The U.S. Department of Energy estimated recoverable reserves at 600 million tons. More important than these reserve figures is the ability to build efficient mining facilities, for it is very difficult to mine coal if it is deposited in secluded or harsh mountainous areas. In other words, it would be hard to guarantee economic feasibility if the costs to mine coal far exceeded the produced energy output.

Coal Production
North Korean coal reserves are known to be mostly anthracite coal. Lignite coals are also produced. However, North Korea imports cokes for utilization by the steel industry. As in other sectors of the economy, coal production in North Korea recorded 33 million tons in 1990 at its highest level. Then it dropped to the bottom level of 18 million tons in 1998, and gradually increased to reach 22 million tons in 2004, which is about 68% of its peak production level.

<Table III-1> Coal Production of North Korea

(Unit: Thousand M/T)

Year	1990	1991	1992	1993	1994	1995	1996
Amount	33,150	31,100	29,200	27,100	25,400	23,700	21,000
Year	1997	1998	1999	2000	2001	2002	2003
Amount	20,600	18,600	21,200	22,500	23,100	21,900	22,300

Source: The Bank of Korea <http://www.bok.or.kr/template/main/html/index.jsp?tbl=tbl_ FM0000000066_CA0000000701>.

In the past, North Korea exported high calorie coals to neighboring countries such as China and Japan. Recently, however, the export of coal has nearly been suspended due to decreased production. For example, North Korea exported around 2 million tons of coal to China and Japan in the past; now it is estimated to be around 500 thousand tons.

Electricity Industry

Electricity Policy
In the 1950s, North Korea's electricity production policy focused on the maintenance and restoration of the existing facilities built by the Japanese during the colonial period. North Korea tried to maintain the Abrok River hydroelectric plant system in the 1950s. At the same time, it tried to restore war-torn hydroelectric power plants with the help of China and Russia. The former Soviet Union provided parts and technologies to North Korea in rehabilitating the power plants.

This policy changed in the 1960s toward balanced production using hydroelectricity and thermal power plants. In the 1970s, North Korea tried to expedite construction projects of thermal power plants and targeted thermal power generation as a primary source of electricity. From 1978 to 1984, thermal power generation accounted for 68% of overall electricity production. Later, North Korea planned to produce 100 billion kilowatts of electricity by the end of 1993. However, these production goals were never realized and North Korea continues to experience severe difficulties in supplying electricity.[6]

---

[6] North Korea Economics Forum, *North Korean Energy* (Seoul: Korea Gas Corporation R&D Division, 1997), pp. 74~76 (In Korean).

North Korea tried to overcome chronic power shortages by building small and medium size hydroelectric power plants. Recently, North Korea emphasized the importance of small size power plants in military use as well. The North Korean news agency reported that North Korea achieved remarkable progress in building small and medium size hydroelectric power plants during the last decade.[7]

North Korea then adopted a policy of shift production in almost all sectors of the economy. The North Korean authorities required factories throughout the country to follow a three-shifts-per-day system in running its facilities. The supply level for electricity is decided by the peak time demand. In general, peak time demand occurs during the daytime when most facilities in the factories are running. Thus, North Korea tries to average out the differences between daytime demand and nighttime demand by adopting this three-shift-per-day system.

Electricity Production
Hydroelectric power plant construction in North Korea began during the Japanese colonial period when Japan exploited North Korean territories as a supply base for the purpose of invading the northeast Asian continent. The Japanese built the Supung, Bujeon, and Jangjin hydroelectric power plants using the Abrok River's currents.

As noted above, North Korea attempted to modernize hydroelectric power plants after the Korean War and built thermal power plants.

---

[7] It is estimated that North Korea constructed 1,000 small and medium size hydroelectric power plants in 1999. In 2000, it built about 130 units and 80 units in 2001. However, these construction activities have been gradually decreased more recently. Ministry of Unification, *Small and Medium Size Power Plants of North Korea, MOU* (Ministry of Unification, June 21, 2004) (In Korean).

One of the reasons for the construction of thermal power plants was that hydroelectric power construction required more time. In addition, North Koreans found a rationale to build more thermal power plants because North Korea had ample coal reserves to be used for thermal power generation.

As shown in <Table III-2>, the amount of electric power generation in 1990 was 27.7 billion kilowatts. It decreased to reach the bottom level of 17 billion kilowatts in 1998 and recovered to 20.6 billion kilowatts in 2004. Considering the level of electricity generation in 2004 was only 74% of the 1990 level, we can understand the severe shortage situation in electricity supply in North Korea.

<Table Ⅲ-2> Electric Power Generation of North Korea

(Unit: Billion Kilowatts)

Year	1990	1991	1992	1993	1994	1995	1996
Amount	27.7	26.3	24.7	22.1	23.1	23.0	21.3
Year	1997	1998	1999	2000	2001	2002	2003
Amount	19.3	17.0	18.6	19.4	20.2	19.0	19.6

Source: The Bank of Korea <http://www.bok.or.kr/template/main/html/index.jsp?tbl=tbl_
        FM0000000066_CA0000000701>.

When we compare North Korean electric power generation capacity with South Korea, North Korea's actual electric power generation in 2003 was only about 6% of South Korea. In addition, North Korean had only about 13% of the facilities that South Korea had. We can note from this comparison that North Korea's operating ratio had been low since the early 1990s. As a matter of fact, experts conjecture that only about 20-30% of the North Korean power plants were operational during the 1990s, due to the low supply of coal and outdated facilities. This signifies the need to rehabilitate old facilities in order to augment electric power generation, rather than building new power plants.

It should also be noted here that North Korea still relies more on hydroelectric power generation than on thermal power generation, in spite of its continuous efforts in constructing the latter type of electric power plants.

<Table Ⅲ-3> Electric Power Generation: North and South Korea

	South	North	Total	S/N
Facility (Thousand kW)	5,605	777	6,382	7.2
Amount (Billion kWh, %)	3,224	196	3,420	16.4
Hydro	3,877 (6.9%)	4,812 (61.9%)	8,689	–
Thermal	36,460 (65.1%)	2,960 (38.1%)	39,420	–
Nuclear	15,716 (28%)	–	15,716	–

Source: Korea National Statistical Office, *Comparison of South and North Korean Socio-Economic Data*, 2004, p. 84-87.

By investigating the technical aspects of the North Korean electric power system, we can see that its electric frequency has been maintained at 60 Hz, which is same as South Korea. As the frequencies of China and Russia are 50 Hz, it is necessary to build separate mechanisms to connect North Korea and the two countries. However, North Korea's frequency fluctuations are very severe and would cause significant problems if we were to connect the North Korean power system with South Korea. North Korea maintains power transmission voltages of 60 Kv, 100 Kv, and 220 Kv, while South Korea maintains voltages between 154 Kv and 765 Kv. Thus, it would be necessary to build a transformer if South and North were to connect power systems.

Another problem of the North Korean power system should be

pointed out here. North Korean facilities are so outdated that they produce unstable electric currents. For example, there are 10-20% voltage fluctuations and 10-15% frequency fluctuations. Also, the North Korean power distribution system is in bad condition because power transmission lines are often outdated. This situation results in very inefficient electricity distribution.

Nuclear Energy
North Korea continuously paid attention to the use of nuclear energy because natural uranium is deposited in its soil. Uranium ores are deposited in the areas such as Unggi, Heungnam, Pyungwon, and Pyungsan. Reserves are estimated to be approximately 26 million tons. North Korea established a nuclear department at Kimchak Technical College. In 1956, North Korea concluded a treaty with the former Soviet Union regarding nuclear energy use. In 1962, North Korea began to construct 2 MW experimental nuclear reactors with the help of the former Soviet Union. In 1985, North Korea made a plan to build 4 units of 440 Thousand KW nuclear power plants with the former Soviet Union. However, this plan was not realized because of the collapse of the Soviet Union and North Korea's economic difficulty. More recent nuclear energy developments in North Korea will be investigated further in the following section.

Oil Industry

The level of North Korean oil consumption has been maintained at about five to ten percent of total energy consumption. As South Korea imports all of its oil supply from overseas, North Korea imports oil from Russia and China. As shown in <Table III-4>, North Korea's major oil supplier has been China. North Korea imported 1100 thousand tons of oil from China in 1991 and it dropped to the bottom level of 317 thousand tons in 1999. Its total oil import figures show the same trends.

North Korea imported oil from China and Russia at a friendly price until early the 1990s. When Russia began Perestroika in the late 1980s, it demanded the market price instead of a low price based on barter trade. Russia also asked to receive hard currency instead of barter trade goods. Thus, oil imports from Russia have drastically decreased since the late 1980s. China, on the other hand, maintained a barter trade system with North Korea for a little longer than Russia. China provided North Korea with 1.5 million tons of

<Table Ⅲ-4> Oil Imports of North Korea

(Unit: Thousand Tons)

	1991	1992	1993	1994	1995	1996	1997
China	1100	1100	1050	830	1020	936	506
Thailand	–	–	–	–	–	–	–
Libya	–	200	100	80	80	–	–
Yemen	–	–	–	–	–	–	600
Iran	750	220	210	–	–	–	–
Russia	40	–	–	–	–	–	–
Syria	–	–	–	–	–	–	–
Total	1890	1520	1360	910	1100	936	1106
	1998	1999	2000	2001	2002	2003	2004
China	503	317	389	579	472	574	532
Thailand	–	–	–	–	–	–	81
Libya	53	–	–	–	–	–	–
Yemen	–	–	–	–	–	–	–
Iran	–	–	–	–	–	–	–
Russia	–	–	–	–	125	–	–
Syria	53	–	–	–	–	–	–
Total	609	317	389	579	597	574	613

Source: KOTRA <http://www.globalwindow.org/front/nk04/nk04_view.jsp?seqNo=933>.

oil at 1/2 price before 1990 based on a barter trade system. North Korea paid the oil costs by exporting coal and cement. China raised the price of oil from 58 dollars in 1989 to 126 dollars in 1990, when the market price of Chinese oil was 131 dollars. At the same time, China increasingly demanded hard currency payments since the early 1990s. However, more importantly, China has never completely cut its oil exports in spite of North Korea's inability to pay. North Korea limits oil consumption to the operation of vehicles and factories because coal can be used for heating and cooking. North Korea has two oil refineries: Seungri Chemical Factory and Bongwha Chemical Factory. The former has refining capacity of 2 million tons per year and the latter, 150 million tons.

North Korea was provided heavy fuel oil by KEDO under the Geneva Agreed Framework between 1995 and 2002. As <Table III-5> shows, KEDO's heavy fuel oil accounted for 39.6% of the total oil supply and 9.1% of the total power generation in North

<Table Ⅲ-5> Ratio of KEDO Heavy Fuel Oil in North Korea[8]

(Unit: %)

	KEDO HFO/Primary	KEDO HFO/Total Oil	KEDO/Power Generation
1995	0.9	13.5	2.5
1996	3.1	34.5	9.0
1997	3.4	49.2	9.6
1998	3.5	35.4	10.3
1999	3.3	56.2	9.3
2000	3.2	44.3	9.4
2001	3.0	39.6	9.1

Source: Kyungsul Kim, *North Korean Energy Problems* (KEEI, 2003), p. 120.

---

[8] This table is borrowed from the following research monograph. Kyungsul Kim, *North Korean Energy Problems* (Gyonggido: Korea Energy Economics Institute, 2003), p. 120 (In Korean).

Korea as of 2001. KEDO's HFO was the only source for oil pow-ered thermal plants during the period. However, this provision of HFO was suspended at the end of 2002. This signifies that North Korea has been vulnerable to severe shortages in its oil supply since 2002. It also implies that China has likely strengthened its position as an oil supplier since then.

Chapter Four

Issues and Problems of North Korean Energy Sector

North Korean energy problems are related to several facets of economics and politics because North Korea maintains unique forms of governance in dealing with its economy. At the same time, North Korean energy problems are intertwined with international concerns, as shown in the process of dealing with North Korea's nuclear development. The current section begins with an analysis of the structural causes of the North Korean energy problems followed by related issues of concern. It also attempts to identify international issues surrounding North Korean energy.

Structural Causes

Disruption in Production Cycles

As shown in the above sections, the North Korean energy industry has been operating with severely reduced supplies in every category. With coal production, North Korean coal mines lost economic efficiency even though North Korea is endowed with abundant coal due to the following reasons. North Korea relied heavily on the manual laborers to dig coal mines. This high dependence on manual labor became one of the reasons for modernizing mining facilities. North Korean mines used to mobilize labor workers because it was the easiest way of increasing productivity. However, this old style of mining gradually lost economic productivity as mines were getting deeper and as high quality coals were being depleted. In order to increase declining productivity, North Korea should have made more efforts to mechanize mining facilities with the introduction of modern equipment. However, North Korea did not have enough capital to import modernized mining equipment from overseas.

The second reason for the decreasing production of coal stemmed from the deforestation of North Korea. North Korea promoted cultivation of mountains in order to increase food production, which, in turn, caused severe deforestation. North Korean mines had less difficulty in getting wood pillars to build galleries in the 1960s and 1970s. As deforestation has spread throughout the country, it became more difficult to provide wood to the coal mines, which in turn caused low coal production.

Third, the low production of coal can be attributed to low electricity generation because North Korean thermal power plants relied on coal. Low electricity production brought about severe problems in running mine equipment factories. The equipment producing factories could not provide mines with new parts indispensable for running coal mines. The low electricity supply also caused problems in transportation since North Korean railroads rely on electricity. Transportation became another problematic factor in meeting the demands of coal mines for supply parts.

The causes of the electricity supply problems are noted here as follows. First, North Korean electric power generation depends highly on hydroelectric power plants. Hydroelectric power plants are influenced by climate fluctuations. Thus, it would be very hard to maintain consistent levels of electric power generation if natural disasters such as droughts or floods occurred. Indeed, natural disasters caused many of the problems in the North Korean energy sector during the 1990s. It should also be noted here that the above mentioned deforestation problem worsened the impact of floods in the mid 1990s in North Korea.

Second, almost all thermal power plants use coal to generate electricity. The decreasing production of coal attributed to the record low level of electricity generation in the mid 1990s. Unless North Korea changes its policy of high dependence on oil, it will be difficult to overcome fundamental problems of supply and demand in the energy sector.

Third, North Korean thermal power plants were constructed with the help of the former Soviet Union and the East European countries. North Korea could not receive spare parts from these countries after the collapse of the socialist bloc in the early 1990s. This situation aggravated North Korea's electric generation capacity because it could not renovate or repair power plants.

Fourth, an inefficient and outmoded transmission and distribution system also attributed to the low electricity supply in North Korea. North Korea relies on old methods in its transmission and distribution system in sending electricity from the producing point to the final end users. Therefore, it shows severe vulnerability to accidents, such as power outages, and is inefficient in maintaining frequencies.

This situation is also one of the causes for the low factory operating ratio.

Inappropriate Governmental Policies
As discussed in the previous sections, North Korea maintained its policy of self-reliance under the Juche ideology. Juche ideology requires energy sector planners to make plans to mobilize domestically available sources and to limit foreign imports. In order to maintain consistent levels of energy supply, however, it is necessary to evenly distribute energy sources for fuel consumption. In other words, the high dependence on coal and hydroelectric power were the results of Juche ideology. Such energy sector imbalances have caused problems in the past, and continue to cause present and future problems.

The North Korean economy is centrally planned and controlled by the central authorities. This type of national economic management often results in inefficient use of energy resources, rigid bureaucratic control of energy production, and arbitrary decision-making and priorities regarding energy consumption in North Korea. For example, the North Korean transmission and distribution system was supposed to manage a complex grid of 62 power plants, 58 substations, and 11 regional transmission and dispatching centers. This system is controlled by the Electric Power Production and Dispatching and Control Center in Pyongyang. However, the central authority lacked direct access to the basic data from power plants and substations. The authorities did not have direct readouts of measurements such as voltage, current, active power, and frequency, nor access to status indicators such open/close conditions of circuit breaker or switch positions.[9] Hippel and Hayes pointed out problems in energy sector management in North Korea as follows:[10]

The fragmentation of institutional responsibility in the energy sector inhibits efforts to upgrade the DPRK's energy systems in general, and the electricity generation and T&D systems in particular. More than a dozen agencies are involved in the electric sector, but there is no single institution in North Korea that is fully responsible for electricity systems operations, energy analysis related to electricity production and consumption, integrated planning, and management.

Another factor affecting the energy situation in North Korea would be the military sector prioritization policy. North Korea, even in the midst of severe economic downturns, gave priorities in maintaining the military sector. Thus scarce economic resources were first used by the military sector, and this inhibited economic recovery. We could speculate the same happened in running the energy industry, causing problems in energy sector development.

North Korea experienced economic problems most severely in the mid 1990s. The North Korean economy nearly collapsed and almost every sector of the economy was in terrible condition. Once the national economy entered this kind of economic situation, every sector of the economy malfunctioned and any single sector problem could easily cause chain reactions in the other sectors of the economy. When the floods hit the already debilitated North Korean economy in the mid 1990s, North Korea was not at all prepared because of Kim Il-Sung's death and the following succession struggles by Kim Jong-Il. As a result, the whole country suffered from food shortages, and people living in rural areas experienced near famine conditions. We could understand that nearly all workers

---

9 David F. Von Hippel and Peter Hayes, "DPRK Energy Sector: Current Status and Scenarios for 2000 and 2005," Paper prepared for the conference, *Economic Integration of the Korean Peninsula* (Washington, D.C., September 5~6, 1997), p. 11~12.
10 *Ibid*, p. 12.

lost their confidence in their workplace at that time. Whereas high worker moral boosted the North Korean economy in the past, the low moral aggravated North Korea's economic problems. This vicious cycle tended to appear more evidently in the coal mines because they were located in remote areas and in the high mountains.

Related Issues of Concern

Nuclear Development
North Korea began nuclear development in the mid 1960s with the help of the former Soviet Union. North built a research reactor, initially 2 kilowatts, later upgraded to 8 kilowatts, at Yongbyon. In the 1980s, North Korea constructed 30 MW gas-cooled reactors, which are graphite-moderated and capable of using natural uranium. North Korea also constructed a reprocessing facility, which can produce weapons-grade plutonium from the spent fuel from the reactor.

North Korea began operation of a 5 megawatts reactor in 1987. This reactor can produce about 6 kilograms of plutonium annually, which is estimated to make a single atomic bomb. North Korea shut down the facility for 70 days in 1989 and the United States intelligence believes that North Korea removed fuel rods for reprocessing into plutonium in order to manufacture a nuclear bomb. In 1994, North Korea again shut down the reactor and removed about 8,000 fuel rods, which could be reprocessed into enough plutonium (25-30 kilograms) for 4-6 nuclear weapons.[11]

---

[11] Larry A. Niksch, "North Korea's Nuclear Weapons Program," *CRS Issue Brief for Congress* (Washington, D.C.: Congressional Research Service, August 31, 2005), p. 8.

These North Korean activities alarmed the international community. After a series of negotiations, North Korea and the United States concluded an agreement in 1994, named the Agreed Framework regarding nuclear development of North Korea. As part of the agreement, North Korea was to be supplied with two Light Water Reactors (LWRs) of the Korean Standard Nuclear Plant Model with a capacity of approximately 1,000 megawatts each in exchange for abolishing its graphite moderated nuclear research reactors and receiving nuclear inspections by the International Atomic Energy Agency (IAEA). Then the Korean Peninsula Energy Development Organization (KEDO) was founded to pursue the above projects.[12] In addition, KEDO was supposed to provide North Korea with 500,000 metric tons of heavy fuel oil, which began in 1995. After James Kelly, Assistant Secretary for East Asia and Pacific Affairs of State Department of the U.S., returned from his trip to North Korea in the fall of 2002, the so-called second nuclear crisis occurred. And KEDO stopped its delivery of heavy fuel oil to North Korea at the end of 2002.

In order to settle the second North Korean nuclear crisis, Six Party Talks have been held in Beijing since 2003 and have recently announced the Joint Statement. Among the contents of the Joint Statement of September 19, 2005, the following texts concerns North Korea's nuclear development.

> The six parties unanimously reaffirmed that the goal of the six-party talks is the verifiable denuclearization of the Korean Peninsula in a peaceful manner. The DPRK (Democratic People's Republic of

---

[12] KEDO was created in March 9, 1995 to implement the 1994 US-DPRK Agreed Framework. KEDO has 13 members: Argentina, Australia, Canada, Czech Republic, Chile, the European Atomic Energy Community (EURATOM), Indonesia, Japan, New Zealand, Poland, Republic of Korea, the United States, and Uzbekistan.

Korea) committed to abandoning all nuclear weapons and existing nuclear programs and returning at an early date to the treaty on the nonproliferation of nuclear weapons and to IAEA (International Atomic Energy Agency) safeguards....

The DPRK stated that it has the right to peaceful uses of nuclear energy. The other parties expressed their respect and agreed to discuss at an appropriate time the subject of the provision of light-water reactor to the DPRK....

The six parties undertook to promote economic cooperation in the fields of energy, trade and investment, bilaterally and/or multilaterally. China, Japan, ROK, Russia and the U.S. stated their willingness to provide energy assistance to the DPRK. The ROK reaffirmed its proposal of July 12, 2005, concerning the provision of 2 million kilowatts of electric power to the DPRK.

It is well known that nuclear energy provides faster solutions to energy deficient countries. And this line of logic was reflected in the contents of the Agreed Framework between North Korea and the U.S. when the latter agreed to provide the former with Light Water Reactors (LWRs). Of course, the provision of LWRs to North Korea had another important purpose, namely, the dismantlement of North Korea's nuclear weapons program. In this sense, the current negotiations among the six parties to solve the North Korean nuclear problems makes us rethink the peaceful use of nuclear energy. Even though the above statement includes very strict conditions, the six parties agreed to grant the right of peaceful nuclear energy use by North Korea. Another important point is that the five parties showed willingness to provide energy assistance to North Korea. As a matter of fact, the North Korean nuclear issue has been brought about by North Korea's actions to develop nuclear weapons. However, during the course of managing North Korean nuclear problems, it encompasses the whole aspect of nuclear uses and non-proliferation. First, North Koreans questioned the very legitimacy of the Non-Proliferation Treaty by withdrawing unilaterally. Second, North Koreans showed a power of brinkmanship diplomacy in the sense that it dragged negotiations to the verge of military conflict. Third, North Koreans earned concessions from the hegemonic power via the nuclear development program. Thus the North Korean nuclear development activities and the following negotiations among the six parties have significant impact on North Korea's energy security.

Survival of the Regime
North Korea has long been preoccupied with the concept of regime survival since the collapse of the socialist bloc in the early 1990s. And its concern was amplified when Kim Il-Sung died. After Kim Il-Sung's death, North Korea concentrated its efforts on maintaining the regime as it had been under the former leadership era, while showing little changes in its attitude in recent years. Along the course of its transition since the early 1990s, North Korea has continuously demanded that the U.S. open up direct bilateral talks. At the same time, North Korea has defined the U.S. as its major enemy. Ironically enough, however, North Korea considers the U.S. to be the most important nation in guaranteeing its survival.

This thinking was reflected in the recent joint statement of the Six Party Talks as follows.

> The United States affirmed that it has no nuclear weapons on the Korean Peninsula and has no intention to attack or invade the DPRK with nuclear or conventional weapons....
> The DPRK and the United States undertook to respect each other's sovereignty, exist peacefully together and take steps to normalize their relations subject to their respective bilateral policies.

Actually, the U.S. provided North Korea with a negative security guarantee when the Agreed Framework was concluded in 1994. This signified that North Korea would not take a big step toward opening-up its economy unless it felt that the regime would be maintained by the North Korean leadership. Because of this, North Korea has been hesitant about adopting a market economy in an earnest manner until recently. This fact hampers the recovery of the North Korean economy in general, and the energy industry in particular.

Development of North-South Korean Economic Relations

South and North Korea have been divided for 60 years. Before their separation, the two political entities had been one nation for a long time. Subsequently, South and North Korean's hope for reunification cannot be explained in one word, and South Korea would be the most reliable partner and source of help for the North Korean economic recovery. In this vein, future South-North Korean relations would have deep bearings on the recovery of North Korea's energy industry. In fact, South Korea has continuously made an effort to build a South-North economic community since the early 1990s. Now, tens of thousands of tourists have already visited Mt. Kumgang via a land route. And South Korean firms operate its factories in the Gaesung industrial complex located in North Korea. There exist factors behind South-North Korean economic exchanges and cooperation.

One of the most important factors that have promoted South-North Korean economic exchanges and cooperation would be South Korea's willingness to help North Korea. As indicated above, South Korea has taken policy measures to expand its economic interactions with North Korea even though the latter has not responded favorably. South Korea's willingness comes from its judgments that it cannot leave North Korea as it is, and that South Korea should enhance the well-being of the North Korean people. Thus South Korea has tried to provide North Korea with opportunities that would contribute to overcoming its economic difficulty. South Korea also wants to mitigate North Korean hostility through economic cooperation. This is based on the belief that economically close political systems are less prone to fight against each other. In other words, South Korea is expecting peaceful effects from its economic exchanges.

In contrast, North Korea's willingness to perform economic exchanges with the South originates primarily from economic calculations. North Korea is in dire need of hard currency to activate its economic revival program under its own terms. And South Korea may be the only source of hard currency for North Korea, as the international community considers North Korea a bankrupt country. Under these circumstances, North Korea reluctantly accepts South Korea's call for economic cooperation, but with strict conditions - economic cooperation packages should not affect the North Korean system. Thus, North Korea allows limited South Korean firms to operate businesses on its soil only if they do not influence the North Korean people and system.

There exist facilitating factors such as common language and geographical proximity. These factors could easily be transformed into economic factors. When we consider economic cooperation among the nations of Northeast Asia, North Korean participation is almost a prerequisite for the smooth flow of goods and services in the region. Once North Korea opens up its borders to South Korea and China, and allows free movement of goods and services, the

Northeast Asian region will become more dynamic, and regional countries will have the opportunity to achieve mutual economic prosperity.

One of the most advanced economic cooperation projects between the North and the South would be construction of the Gaeseong Industrial Complex (GIC). Gaeseong is located quite close to Seoul, the capital city of South Korea. Indeed, it is only 60 kilometers from Seoul and 160 kilometers from Pyongyang, the capital city of North Korea. Hyundai Corporation of South Korea initiated the GIC project in 2000. A model site has been completed and there are plans to complete the first phase of construction by the end of 2006. In order to meet the demands for the factories in GIC, South Korea's Electric Power Corporation (KEPCO) has sent 15,000 kilowatts of electricity to the model site since March 16, 2005. KEPCO plans to send 100,000 kilowatts to the completed first phase site in order to meet the demands for the South Korean factories which are planned to start operation in the end of 2006.[13]

Northeast Asian Energy Cooperation

Since North Korea is located in the heart of the Northeast Asian region, it is worthwhile to analyze current situations of Northeast Asian energy cooperation. Six Northeast Asian countries[14] con-

---

[13] Model site has already been opened and the first phase of development aims at 3.3 million square meters by the end of 2006. Second phase of construction is planned to be finished by the end of 2009 and includes 8.3 million square meters of factory site and 3.3 square meters of support city. The final phase of industrial complex construction will be completed by the end of 2012 with 18.2 million square meters of factory sites and 6.6 million square meters of support city. Ministry of Unification, *Gaeseong Idustrial Complex Guide* (Seoul: Ministry of Unification, Office of Gaeseong Industrial Complex Project, 2005).

[14] China, Japan, Russia, South Korea, North Korea, Mongolia.

sumed about 25% of the world energy in 2000 as shown in <Table IV-1>.[15] China leads the energy consumption among the six countries even though its per capita energy consumption remains at a low level compared with the other industrialized countries. The most important implication from this table would be the fact that China's consumption already exceeded that of Japan and Russia.

<Table IV-1> Energy Situation of Northeast Asia

2000	Primary Energy (Million TOE)	Per Capita Energy (TOE)
South Korea	192.9	4.08
Japan	558.7	4.40
China	950.0	0.75
Russia	612.0	4.21
Mongolia	2.6	1.03
North Korea	15.7	0.71
NEA	2,332	1.44
World	9,179	1.51

Source: Jinwoo Kim, "Energy Security of Northeast Asia," *Energy Challenges in Northeast Asia and Project Proposal in 2004* (KEEI-IEA, 2004).

When we look at energy consumption according to the types of energy sources, regional countries rely on different sources. As shown in <Table IV-2>, coal accounts for 62% of China's energy consumption, followed by oil (27.6%). This heavy dependence on coal worries China and neighboring countries due to the adverse impact on the Northeast Asian environment.

Japan, on the other hand, relies heavily on oil (48%). Natural gas

---

[15] Jinwoo Kim, "Energy Security of Northeast Asia: Current State, Energy Demand/ Supply Projection and Investment Needs," Paper prepared for the KEEI-IEA Joint Conference on *Energy Challenges in Northeast Asia and Project Proposals in 2004* (Seoul: KEEI-IEA, March 16~17, 2004).

<Table Ⅳ-2> Energy Mix of China

(Unit: Million TOE, %)

	Primary Energy Consumption	Share
Oil	231.9	27.6
Natural Gas	24.9	3.0
Coal	520.6	62.0
Nuclear Energy	4.0	0.5
Hydroelectricity	58.3	6.9
Total	839.7	100.0

Source: *Ibid.*

(13.8%) and nuclear energy (14.1%) also occupy significant portions. Japan has long been an importer of oil and natural gas. South Korea, like Japan, imports almost all of its energy sources. South Korea ranks 3rd in importing oil and 2nd in importing coal and LNG. South Korea spends 33.7 US billion dollars in importing energy from overseas.

<Table Ⅳ-3> Energy Mix of South Korea and Japan

(Unit: Million TOE, %)

	Primary Energy Consumption		Share	
	South Korea	Japan	South Korea	Japan
Oil	103.1	247.2	52.6	48.0
Natural Gas	20.8	71.1	10.6	13.8
Coal	45.7	103.0	23.3	20.0
Nuclear Energy	25.4	72.7	13.0	14.1
Hydroelectricity	0.9	20.4	0.5	4.0
Total	195.9	514.5	100.0	100.0

Source: *Ibid.*

With the high economic growth of the region, energy consumption in Northeast Asia has been increasing quite rapidly and this trend is expected to continue.[16] First, it is forecasted that China's demand would grow at an annual rate of 4.7% and South Korea's demand at 2.8% between 1999 and 2020, compared with the forecasted world average growth rate of 2.2%. Second, three Northeast Asian countries (China, Japan, South Korea) are heavily dependent on oil: Japan ranks 2nd, China ranks 3rd, and South Korea ranks 6th in world consumption of oil. Third, these three countries import oil from outside of the region. In 1999, 76% of oil was imported from the Middle East. Fourth, the high dependency on coal and oil generally produces more environmental problems.

It should be noted here that the growing demand and energy mix would create the following tensions in the region. The first point is related with sea-lane security in the Middle East. As regional countries are highly dependent on oil imports from the Middle East, national leaders will be tempted to increase its sphere of influence in the Southeast Asian region. Another point that should be made here is that ever-increasing pollution problems of China would threaten neighboring countries, especially South Korea. China would want to maintain current levels of economic development in at least the foreseeable future. Without proper and coordinated efforts, environmental problems will surely damage China and its neighboring countries.

Another area deserving attention is the supply side of the equation, as Russia has oil and gas to be explored. Eastern Siberia is presumed to have oil reserves of 21.4 billion barrels.[17] Oil and gas

---

[16] *Ibid.*

[17] In the early 1930s, when the exploration of Eastern Siberia began, most reserves in this area were known to be gas reserves, but, since 1969, after Yaraktinskoye field was found, other oil reserves have been actively developed such as Yurubecheno-Tokhomskaya field in 1982 and Kovyktinskoye field in 1987. Hoon Paik, *A Study on Harmonization between Multilateral and Bilateral Energy Cooperation in Northeast*

fields are located in three regions: Krasnoyarsk Krai (12.2 billion barrels), Irkutsk Oblast (1.7 billion barrels), and Sakha Republic (2.4 billion barrels). There had been several suggestions about the construction of pipelines from Eastern Siberia to regional countries as follows.[18]

Irkutsk: 3 routes
Russia-China-South Korea
Russia-Mongolia-China-North Korea-South Korea
Russia-China-North Korea-South Korea

Yakutsk: 2 Routes
Russia-China-North Korea
Russia-North Korea-South Korea

Sakhalin: 3 Routes
Russia-China-North Korea-South Korea
Russia-North Korea-South Korea
Russia-China-South Korea

These pipeline projects would require long-term development and vast amounts of investment. However, at the core of these pipeline alternatives lies North Korea. Without a sincere cooperation from the North Korean government authorities and confidence from the regional countries, it would be unimaginable to build pipelines through North Korean territory.

Asia (New Asia Economy and Technology Federation, 2004).
[18] East Siberia oil pipelines are also suggested as Angarsk-Daqing and Angarsk-Nakhodka

<Figure IV-1> Alternative Gas Pipelines in Northeast Asia

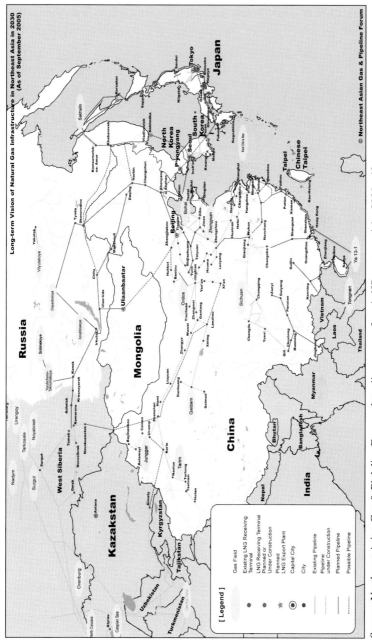

Source: Northeast Asian Gas & Pipeline Forum <http://www.nagpf.org/pdf/Longtermvision2030.pdf>.

\<Figure Ⅳ-2\> Alternative Electric Power Link in Northeast Asia

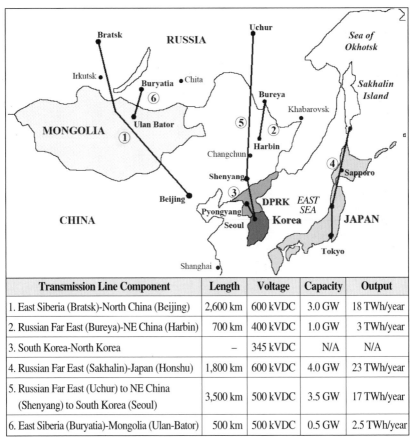

Transmission Line Component	Length	Voltage	Capacity	Output
1. East Siberia (Bratsk)-North China (Beijing)	2,600 km	600 kVDC	3.0 GW	18 TWh/year
2. Russian Far East (Bureya)-NE China (Harbin)	700 km	400 kVDC	1.0 GW	3 TWh/year
3. South Korea-North Korea	–	345 kVDC	N/A	N/A
4. Russian Far East (Sakhalin)-Japan (Honshu)	1,800 km	600 kVDC	4.0 GW	23 TWh/year
5. Russian Far East (Uchur) to NE China (Shenyang) to South Korea (Seoul)	3,500 km	500 kVDC	3.5 GW	17 TWh/year
6. East Siberia (Buryatia)-Mongolia (Ulan-Bator)	500 km	500 kVDC	0.5 GW	2.5 TWh/year

Source: Asia Pacific Energy Research Centre, *Electric Power Grid Interconnections in the APEC Region 2004* (APERC, 2004), p. 9, <http://www.ieej.or.jp/aperc/pdf/GRID_COMBINED_DRAFT.pdf>.

Chapter Five

Cooperative Projects for Energy Sector Development

The current research has identified the factors behind North Korean energy situation in the previous section as follows. First, there certainly exist problematic factors which have debilitated the North Korean energy sector. Most problems stem from economic difficulties: (a) disrupted supply and demand channels and (b) inappropriate governmental policies. Related issues of concern were also discussed: (a) the crisis-prone nuclear development program, (b) preoccupation of leadership with regime survival, and (c) the development of North-South economic relations. The future paths of Northeast Asian energy cooperation will influence North Korea's energy development, with the latter affecting the former as indicated in the previous section. In other words, North Korean energy sector difficulties have originated from their own mismanagement, but at the same time, the problems have been aggravated by the international political and economic turbulence. In this vein, solutions to North Korean energy sector problems should be based on comprehensive thinking, which encompass economic factors and political considerations. The current section begins with the objectives of the suggestions for the North Korean energy sector development. Then it shall suggest cooperative measures based on the several assumptions and principles.

Objectives

As we have seen from the previous section regarding the supply and demand structure of the energy sector in North Korea, three fundamental problems were identified: chronic shortage of supply, excessive dependence on coal, and outmoded infrastructure. Indeed, the current level of North Korea's energy supply is only about 60-70% of the 1990 level. When we consider the energy supply in 1990 was not enough to support economic growth, these figures help put North Korea's catastrophic situation into perspective. Thus, the first and foremost goal should be the achievement of increased supply.

At the same time, it is necessary to try to reduce the high dependence on coal because relying on a single energy resource would easily result in serious problems of supply if production of the primary resource fluctuated. As North Korea has developed more and more coal mines, productivity and the quality of coal has dropped drastically. And North Koreans have lost opportunities to learn higher energy development technologies because coal mines and coal fired power plants were built 20-30 years ago. If North Korea had turned their attention to creating a balanced energy supply structure, it would have been more beneficial in developing its energy industry. In this vein, the second objective of North Korean energy sector development should be the achievement of a balanced supply structure.

North Korea has allocated much of its resources for the maintenance of a huge military sector since its foundation. As indicated previously, this became one of the fundamental reasons behind the current economic, as well as energy sector, difficulties. It is necessary for North Korea to pay more attention to improve the well-being of its citizens. Without proper power consumption by ordinary citizens, it would be hard to imagine a normal course of economic development. This fact applies to the supply/demand mechanisms of the energy sector as well. As noted above, North Korean people used mountain trees for cooking and heating during the 1990s, which was one of the causes of severe deforestation. Thus, it is necessary to increase the energy supply to households in order to improve overall energy supply/demand structure.

Along with the three economic objectives above, it is necessary for us to set related political goals since the North Korean energy sector difficulties were largely caused by international political turbulence during the 1990s. It should be noted here that the North Korean economic hardship had been aggravated by its isolation from the international community. The North Korean nuclear weapons development program and resultant crises made North Korea a focal point in security issues in Northeast Asia. However, North Korea became more isolated in its economic exchanges with the capitalist world because the attention from the international community surrounding its nuclear weapons program created a fundamentally conflict-ridden and negative North Korean national image. No country in the world would want to trade with a militarily hostile country. North Korea should make more of an effort in creating a more peaceful image with the international community in order to receive outside help. Thus, it is necessary to prioritize a complete dismantlement of the nuclear weapons program in pursuing

North Korea's energy sector development. This goal applies to North Korea's relations with South Korea. In other words, developmental assistance to North Korea in energy sector should be based on the objectives that it would contribute to the peaceful unification progress and to the stability of international relations in Northeast Asia.

Cooperative Projects

Basic Assumptions and Guiding Principles
With the above goals in mind, the current section attempts to provide cooperative projects for ameliorating North Korea's energy sector difficulties. In order to systematically figure out alternatives, it is necessary to mention the basic assumptions governing the following suggestions and the principles guiding various projects.

As many experts have difficulty in predicting North Korea's future, it is not easy to portray North Korea's energy futures in a scientific way. Most analyses suffered from scarce reliable data and, more importantly, could not include political and security variables. In this vein, the current research adds international political factors in order to strengthen rationales behind the following suggestions. It also tries to include possible attitudinal changes of North Korea's economic policies in a certain direction in order to provide more consistent arguments about the following cooperative measures.

As discussed above, one of the most important factors in deciding North Korea's future is the six party process. Indeed, any plan for future energy assistance to North Korea will be directly affected by the resultant progress of the six party talks. It is necessary to delineate energy related progresses here as follows. First, the five parties

- the U.S., China, Russia, Japan and South Korea - would begin the shipment of heavy fuel oil. Second, South Korea would begin sending electricity to North Korea after the construction of transmission facilities is completed. Third, the provision of LWRs could be revived if North Korean nuclear development related facilities are completely dismantled.

Along with the six party processes, North Korea's internal development would influence the future paths of the energy industry. North Korea showed a rather lukewarm attitude towards the opening-up of its economy during the 1990s. This trend has changed a little since 2002, when North Korea implemented economic management improvement measures. Thus it is reasonable to assume that North Korea will gradually adopt more market mechanisms in the management of its national economy and in its foreign trade dealings. This kind of attitudinal change should be taken more seriously because outside help alone will never solve the fundamental North Korean energy sector problems.

In order to effectively achieve the aforementioned objectives in developing North Korean energy industry, it is necessary to execute systematic plans in a coordinated manner. In relation with the economic and political objectives delineated above, it is necessary for us to coordinate South Korean aid plans with international activities, especially those of Northeast Asian regional countries. In other words, South Korea needs to take initiatives in helping North Korea to recover from the current difficulties and to be prepared to provide rationales for such initiatives. At the same time, South Korea needs to coordinate with Northeast Asian regional countries. Thus, actual plans to improve North Korea's energy sector would have to be made by multilateral discussions and/or institutions. In this way, we can avoid unnecessary suspicions from North Korea about unification by absorption from South Korea. This approach will also contribute to the peace building processes of the region.

The second guideline for North Korea's energy sector development assistance is that it should be future-oriented in nature. South Korea has promoted a building of the North-South Economic Community since the early 1990s to meet the various future challenges of ultimate unification on the Korean peninsula. In order to economically manage the unification process, it is necessary to increase the economic capacity of North Korea because a narrowed gap between the North and the South would decrease unification cost. And this rule also applies to the improvement projects of the energy sector. In this vein, it is important to modernize North Korea's energy related facilities and to educate North Korean technicians in more advanced technologies.

In order to execute aid plans more systematically, it is necessary to provide developmental assistance. We have to remember the fact that many developing countries are still living under poor conditions even though they have received significant amounts of money and commodities from international aid agencies. Thus, aid plans for the North Korean energy sector should be made more comprehensively from the beginning. Perhaps we can learn lessons from the past experiences of food aid programs executed in the 1990s. It is necessary to coordinate aid plans among the providing parties. This is especially true in improving the North Korean energy industry because coal production problems have triggered other sectoral problems and have caused a vicious cycle. We should also keep in mind that it would be difficult to guarantee the efficient use of energy if the North Korean electric grid system is not modernized, even after North Korea receives electricity from South Korea and elsewhere.

Cooperative Projects

Institutional Needs
It is necessary to form an institution to handle North Korean energy problems more comprehensively. There exist two international mechanisms related to North Korean energy issues. Even though its existence itself is under question now, KEDO has operated since 1995 with the purpose of coordinating LWR projects and the provision of heavy fuel oil to North Korea. Six party talks provide another forum for discussing North Korea's energy issues, though it has not yet been institutionalized and its focus is more on nuclear issues.

It may be a good idea to organize an international institution to handle North Korean energy issues, with core members being the U.S., China, Russia, Japan, South and North Korea. Membership for such an organization could be open to other interested nations. The first category of broadened membership would include a country such as Mongolia, which belongs to the Northeast Asian region. The second category can be possible energy supply countries located in the Central Asian region. The third group of countries to be considered would be the current members of KEDO, such as Australia and Canada.

The proposed international institution could be named the North Korean Energy Development Center and could perform various functions. It could function as a forum for discussion among the concerned parties. With the initiative of the South Korean government, it could provide opportunities for North Koreans to learn modern technologies of energy sector management. It could also allow North Korea to benefit from the experience of other transitional economies. As the proposed institution would run on a multilateral basis, we could cooperatively find better solutions to North Korean energy problems. At the same time, it could integrate various energy improvement projects in order to gain maximum results.

Suggestions for Improvement Projects
Improving the energy sector of North Korea involves various sectors of the economy and requires considerable time. The current section attempts to suggest projects to be implemented in each of the following three stages. The primary focus of the first stage would be rehabilitating the North Korean energy industry. Upon entering second stage, North Korea could pursue development of the energy industry based on the outcomes of the previous stage. During the third stage, North Korea could further develop energy its industry and achieve practical growth.

• Rehabilitation Stage
The first stage could be referred to as the "Rehabilitation Stage" because the North Korean energy sector has retrogressed during the 1990s. Thus, the foremost task for the North Korean energy improvement plan should be to regain the production level of the early 1990s. In order to achieve this goal, North Korea needs outside help because it does not have the essential resources for rehabilitation. During the rehabilitation stage, the following measures need to be implemented.

The first important step towards North Korean energy development would be a systematic investigation of the current situation. Of course, it would be most helpful if North Koreans were to become participants in such a forum. It is necessary to collect all available information about the North Korean energy industry and compile such data in an integrated manner. Then energy experts, including North Koreans, should discuss optimal ways to enhance the North Korean energy sector. In this vein, the South Korean government needs to play a key role in promoting such activities by supporting international seminars and the exchange of technicians. For example, it is necessary to hold an international seminar on the improvement of the energy sector in North Korea among the experts of North and South Korea, China, and Russia. Then these international seminars could be regularized and become a foundation for a permanent international forum. In this way, North Koreans would have opportunities to learn advanced technologies and management skills.

Second, the most immediate need from the North Korean side would be the renovation of its outmoded facilities. In doing so, initial efforts should be concentrated on the renovation of mining facilities since North Korea is highly dependent on coal as its primary energy source. In other words, it is essential to regain the production level of coal in 1990. Simultaneous efforts should be devoted to the renovation of transportation facilities, especially railroads, because inadequate transportation infrastructure has hindered the smooth flow of the energy supply during the 1990s. Along with the improvement projects for the renovation of the mining and transportation facilities, it is necessary to renovate power plants. North Korean power plants were not supplied with parts during the 1990s. Debilitated power plants resulted in the inefficient use of energy sources and low operating ratios. Perhaps the optimal solution for these debilitated power plants would be the construction of new ones. However, the cost would be high and it would take a long time to achieve such a goal. Thus, as an interim solution, it is necessary to renovate power plants. South Korea could become a participant of such projects. Currently, North Korea renovates its power plants on an ad-hoc basis because it does not have the much needed capital to undergo a comprehensive system renovation. It is necessary to form an international consortium to handle such renovation projects. In this regard, the role of Russia is very important because most of power plants were built with the help of the former Soviet Union. The South Korean government can become a source of project funding and management guidance.

The third project is the provision of electricity to the Gaeseong Industrial Complex as noted in the previous section. In addition to this project, it is necessary to begin construction projects during this stage for the transmission of two million kilowatts of electricity to North Korea. It is forecasted that such a construction project would take at least three years. The South Korean Ministry of Unification recently estimated that it would cost about 6.5 to 11 trillion won for the next nine to thirteen years depending on the results of the negotiation between North Korea and the concerned parties. This figure can be broken into four categories: provision of heavy fuel oil for three years (150 billion won), construction of electricity transmission facilities (1.7 trillion won), electricity provision of 2 million kilowatts for six to ten years (3.9 to 8 trillion won), and a light water nuclear power plant of 2 million kilowatts (700 million to 1 trillion won).[19] As it would require a long time to stabilize the

---

[19] South Korean Ministry of Unification, *Energy Provision to North Korea* (Ministry of Unification, September 22, 2005) (In Korean).

North Korean energy supply, the construction of transmission facilities should be part of the first stage so that actual provision of electricity could begin in the following stage.

As an interim solution for the problems regarding the North Korean nuclear development program, it would be necessary to provide heavy fuel oil in this stage under the assumption that North Korea will show cooperative attitudes towards the decisions made by the Six Party Talks. As noted above, the shipment of heavy fuel oil to North Korea as agreed in the Agreed Framework has stopped since the end of 2002. Thus, North Korea should have a desperate need for heavy fuel oil for electricity generation. In order to restart operation of thermal power plants, North Korea needs heavy fuel oil from the outside world.

• Development Stage
After the North Korean energy industry is restored to produce supply levels equal to that of 1990, it would enter into a development stage in the sense that North Korea further develops its energy production not only in the areas of mining coal, but also electricity. In the previous stage, the North Korean energy supply would have met basic energy demands. However, it would not be sufficient, and North Korea would need to explore ways to advance its economy. Thus North Korea needs to adopt the following projects to increase its energy supply with the help of the outside world.

First, it is necessary to internationalize the issue of South Korea's provision of two million megawatts of electricity to North Korea. The provision of LWRs to North Korea became an international issue, even though it was the result of American-North Korean negotiations. Similarly, the South Korean proposal has already become internationalized because its major contents have been included in a recent joint statement made by the six parties. Thus, it is necessary to open up discussions regarding the electricity provision to North Korea to concerned parties, including the participants of the Six Party Talks and other interested countries.

Second, it is necessary to modernize electricity gridlines throughout the country during this stage in order to adequately transmit produced electricity to the end users. In doing so, international assistance is needed to modernize transmission and distribution systems for the efficient use of electricity.

Third, South Korea could begin to send two million kilowatts of electricity to North Korea with the assumption that the above mentioned projects would have been completed. In fact, it would be efficient to utilize seasonal and daily peak time uses of electricity. South Korea's peak season is summer because of its heavy use of air conditioners during hot weather. In contrast, electricity consumption during winter is relatively lower in South Korea. Thus, it may be a good idea for South Korea to send more electricity during winter time because the North Korean winter climate is much colder than South Korea.

• **Growth Stage**
Upon entering the third stage, the North Korean economy and energy industry may have recovered enough to pursue further growth. Such a situation requires an increased supply of energy to support growing demands made by economic growth. Thus it is necessary to consider the following projects to adequately supply energy to North Korea.

The first project is related to the pipeline construction projects which are currently being discussed by the Northeast Asian countries. For the sake of simplicity, we can propose two pipelines which will use North Korean territory. One line could pass through the western part of North Korea, while the other could pass through the eastern part. As for economic feasibility, the latter is more economical and should be utilized in the long run to provide a supply of energy to South Korea and Japan.

The second project would be the connection of electric grid lines between North Korea and the Russian Far East. The latter area has enough reserves of electricity, as it has access to gas and oil in East Siberia. The only problem is that Russian electric currents are 50 Hz and North Korean currents are 60 Hz. Thus it will be necessary to install a transformer along the borderlines of North Korea and Russia. We can consider the use of Russian energy as a possible source for North Korean energy needs.

The third project could be more controversial because it is related to the use of nuclear energy. As noted above, North Korea's nuclear development program has long been disputed because of its dual usages. North Korea has yet to completely dismantle its existing nuclear weapons development program even though the Six Party Talks resumed and made some progress. We can think of two alternatives here. On the one hand, we could resume the construction of two light water reactors at Sinpo. On the other hand, we could form an international consortium to build other types of nuclear power plants, possibly a Russian model. It would be difficult to predict the future course of North Korea's nuclear development program. The current research suggests resuming the construction of two light water reactors, if it were to be decided and agreed by the six parties.

Chapter Six

Conclusion

North Korea has experienced severe economic problems during the 1990s because of internal as well as external factors. Upon entering the twenty-first century, the North Korean economy has been slowly recovering from its lowest level of economic production. North Korean authorities have also adopted several market-oriented measures in the middle of 2002. In the midst of these recent changes, North Korea is in desperate need of energy in order to support economic recovery. Indeed, energy is indispensable for every country pursuing economic development. The current research analyzed current situations of North Korean energy industries and suggested projects for improving the North Korean energy situation. In implementing such projects, the following points should always be kept in mind.

In order to adequately provide energy assistance to North Korea, it is absolutely necessary for South Korea to maintain the principle of transparency. As North Korea is still largely secluded from the outside world, the South Korean government needs to ask North Korea to provide records of its energy use. At the same time, the South Korean government needs to fully inform its own people regarding the processes of such assistance. This point is very important in an economic sense as well because opaque procedures in helping North Korea in the past have often resulted in failure or discontinuity.

It is necessary to be patient in dealing with North Korea and to maintain a longer-term perspective. We need to understand that the North Korean people, having lived under a centrally planned economy, may have very different attitudes. They probably never imagined the conditions they are experiencing now. The above projects may also require much more time to realize than we anticipate. A more important yardstick for the success of the energy improvement projects may be the direction, not the outcome. In other words, it is necessary for us to keep the projects moving and to try to maintain continuity even though the projects may progress very slowly.

In conclusion, it is necessary for us to keep in mind that South and North Korea were one nation for a long time. We need to prepare for the ultimate reunification, though it is hard to predict the exact time frame. During the course of implementing energy improvement projects, we may be confronted with rather lukewarm, or sometimes harsh, reactions from North Korea and from inside South Korea. However, the goals and measures suggested in this research should be pursued with diligence, patience, and consistency in order to realize a prosperous unified Korea.

Agreement on Supply of a Light-Water Reactor Project to the Democratic People's Republic of Korea Between the Korean Peninsula Energy Development Organization and the Government of the Democratic People's Republic of Korea

The Korean Peninsula Energy Development Organization (hereinafter referred to as "KEDO") and the Government of the Democratic People's Republic of Korea (the Democratic People's Republic of Korea is hereinafter referred to as the "DPRK"),

Recognizing that KEDO is an international organization to finance and supply a light-water reactor project (hereinafter referred to as the "LWR project") to the DPRK as specified in the Agreed Framework between the United States of America and the Democratic People's Republic of Korea of October 21, 1994 (hereinafter referred to as the "U.S.-DPRK Agreed Framework"),

Recognizing that the U.S.-DPRK Agreed Framework and the June 13,1995, U.S.-DPRK Joint Press Statement specify that the U.S. will serve as the principal point of contact with the DPRK for the LWR project, and

Reaffirming that the DPRK shall perform its obligations under the relevant provisions of the U.S.-DPRK Agreed Framework and shall accept the LWR project as specified in the June 13, 1995, U.S.-DPRK Joint Press Statement,

Have agreed as follows :

Article I

Scope off Supply

1. KEDO shall provide the LWR project, consisting of two pressurized

lightwater reactor (LWR) units with two coolant loops and a generating capacity of approximately 1,000 MW(e) each, to the DPRK on a turnkey basis. The reactor model, selected by KEDO, will be the advanced version of U.S.-origin design and technology currently under production.

2. KEDO shall be responsible for the scope of supply for the LWR project, specified in Annex 1 to the Agreement. The DPRK shall be responsible for other tasks and items necessary for the LWR project, specified in Annex 2 to the Agreement.

3. The LWR project shall conform to a set of codes and standards equivalent to those of the IAEA and the U.S. and applied to the reactor model referred to in paragraph 1 of this Article. The set of codes and standards shall apply to the design, manufacture, construction, testing, commissioning, and operation and maintenance of the LWR plants, including safety, physical protection, environmental protection, and storage and disposal of radioactive waste.

Article II

Terms of Repayment

1. KEDO shall finance the cost of the tasks and items specified in Annex 1 to the Agreement to be repaid by the DPRK on a long-term, interest-free basis.

2. The amount to be repaid by the DPRK will be jointly determined by KEDO and the DPRK based on examination by each side of the technical description of the LWR project specified in the commercial supply contract for the LWR project, the fair and reasonable market value of the LWR project, and the contract price payable by KEDO to its contractors and subcontractors under the commercial supply contracts for the tasks and items specified in Annex 1 to the Agreement, the DPRK shall not be responsible for any additional costs, other than those that result from actions by the DPRK or from its failure to take actions for which it is responsible, in which case the repayment amount shall be increased by an amount jointly determined by KEDO and the DPRK, based on actual added cost to the LWR project payable by KEDO.

3. The DPRK shall repay KEDO for each LWR plant in equal, semiannual installments, free of interest, over a 20-year term after completion of each LWR plant, including a three-year grace period beginning upon completion of that LWR plant. The DPRK may pay KEDO in cash, cash equivalents, or through the transfer of goods. In the event that the DPRK pays in cash equivalents or goods (such payment is hereinafter referred to as "in-kind payment"), the value of such in-kind payment shall be determined jointly by KEDO and the DPRK, based on an agreed formula for determining fair and reasonable market price.

4. Details concerning the amount and terms of repayment shall be specified in a separate protocol between KEDO and the DPRK pursuant to the Agreement.

Article III

Delivery Schedule

1. KEDO shall develop a delivery schedule for the LWR project aimed at achieving a completion date of 2003. The schedule of relevant steps to be performed by the DPRK under the U.S.-DPRK Agreed Framework, as specified in Annex 3 to the Agreement, shall be integrated with the delivery schedule for the LWR project with the aim of achieving the performance of such steps by 2003 and the smooth implementation of the LWR project. As specified in the U.S.-DPRK Agreed Framework, the provision of the LWR project and the performance of the steps specified in Annex 3 to the Agreement are mutually conditional.

2. For purposes of the Agreement, "completion" of an LWR plant means completion of performance tests that is satisfactory in accordance with the set of codes and standards specified in Article I(3). Upon completion of each plant, the DPRK shall issue to KEDO a take-over certificate for each respective plant.

3. Details concerning the delivery schedule for the delivery of the LWR project and the performance of the steps specified in Annex 3 to the Agreement, including mutually agreed procedures for any necessary changes and completion of a significant portion of the LWR project as specified in Annex 4 to the Agreement, shall be specified in a separate

protocol between KEDO and the DPRK pursuant to the Agreement.

Article IV

Implementing Arrangements

1. The DPRK may designate a DPRK firm as its agent and authorize the firm to enter into implementing arrangements as necessary to facilitate the LWR project.

2. KEDO shall select a prime contractor to carry out the LWR project and shall conclude a commercial supply contract with this prime contractor. A U.S. firm will serve as program coordinator to assist KEDO in supervising overall implementation of the LWR project, and KEDO will select the program coordinator.

3. KEDO and the DPRK shall facilitate practical arrangements that both sides deem necessary, including efficient contacts and cooperation among the participants in the LWR project, to ensure the expeditious and smooth implementation of the LWR project.

4. Written communications required for the implementation of the Agreement may be executed in the English or Korean languages. Existing documents and data may be used or transmitted in their original languages.

5. KEDO, its contractors and subcontractors shall be permitted to operate offices at the project site and other directly reacted locations such as the nearby port or airport as shall be agreed between KEDO and the DPRK, as the progress of the LWR project may require.

6. The DPRK shall recognize KEDO's independent juridical status and shall accord KEDO and its staff such privileges and immunities in the territory of the DPRK as necessary to carry out the functions entrusted to KEDO. KEDO's juridical status and privileges and immunities shall be specified in a separate protocol between KEDO and the DPRK pursuant to the Agreement.

7. The DPRK shall take steps to protect the safety of all personnel sent to

the DPRK by KEDO, its contractors and subcontractors and their respective property. Appropriate consular protection in conformity with established international practice shall be allowed for all such personnel. Necessary consular arrangements shall be specified in a separate protocol between KEDO and the DPRK pursuant to the Agreement.

8. KEDO shall take steps to ensure that all personnel sent to the DPRK by KEDO, its contractors and subcontractors shall undertake to respect the relevant laws of the DPRK, as shall be agreed between KEDO and the DPRK, and to conduct themselves at all times in a decent and professional manner.

9. The DPRK shall not interfere with the repatriation, in accordance with customs clearance procedures, by KEDO, its contractors and subcontractors of construction equipment and remaining materials from the LWR project.

10. The DPRK shall seek recovery solely from the property and assets of KEDO for the satisfaction of any claims arising under the Agreement or from any of the acts and omissions, liabilities, or obligations of KEDO, its contractors and subcontractors in direct connection with the Agreement, protocols and contracts pursuant to the Agreement.

Article V

Site Selection and Study

1. KEDO shall conduct a study of the preferred Kumho area near Sinpo City, South Hamgyong Province to ensure that the site satisfies appropriate site selection criteria as shall be agreed between KEDO and the DPRK and to identify the requirements for construction and operation of the LWR plants, including infrastructure improvements.

2. To facilitate this study, the DPRK shall cooperate and provide KEDO with access to the relevant available information, including the results for the studies that were performed previously at this site. In the event that such data is not sufficient, KEDO shall make arrangements to obtain additional information or to conduct the necessary site studies.

3. Details concerning site access and the use of the site shall be specified in a separate protocol between KEDO and the DPRK pursuant to the Agreement.

Article VI

Quality assurance and Warranties

1. KEDO shall be responsible for design and implementation of a quality assurance program in accordance with the set of codes and standards specified in Article I(3). The quality assurance program shall include appropriate procedures for design, materials, manufacture and assembly of equipment and components, and quality of construction.

2. KEDO shall provide the DPRK with appropriate documentation on the quality assurance program, and the DPRK shall have the right to participate in the implementation of the quality assurance program, which will include appropriate inspections, tests, commissioning, and review by the DPRK of the results thereof.

3. KEDO shall guarantee that the generation capacity of each LWR plant at the time of completion, as defined in Article III(2), will be approximately 1,000MW(e). KEDO shall guarantee that the major components provided by relevant contractors and subcontractors will be new and free from defects in design, workmanship, and material for a period of two years after completion, but in no event longer than five years after the date of shipment of such major components. The LWR fuel for the initial loading for each LWR plant shall be guaranteed in accordance with standard nuclear industry practice. KEDO shall guarantee that the civil construction work for the LWR project will be free of defects in design, workmanship, and material for a period of two years after completion.

4. Details concerning the provisions of this Article and the content and procedures for issuance and receipt of warranties shall be specified in a separate protocol between KEDO and the DPRK pursuant to the Agreement.

Article VII

Training

1. KEDO shall design and implement a comprehensive training program in accordance with standard nuclear industry practice for the DPRK's operation and maintenance of the LWR plants. Such training shall be held at mutually agreeable locations as soon as practicable. The DPRK shall be responsible for providing a sufficient number of qualified candidates for this program.

2. Details concerning the training program shall be specified in a separate protocol between KEDO and the DPRK pursuant to the Agreement.

Article VIII

Operation and Maintenance

1. KEDO shall assist the DPRK to obtain LWR fuel, other than that provided pursuant to Annex 1 to the Agreement, through commercial contracts with a DPRK-preferred supplier for the useful of the LWR plants.

2. KEDO shall assist the DPRK to obtain spare and wear parts, consumables, special tools, and technical services for the operation and maintenance of the LWR plants, other than those provided pursuant to Annex 1 to the Agreement, through commercial contracts with a DPRK preferred supplier for the useful life of the LWR plants.

3. KEDO and the DPRK shall cooperate to ensure the safe storage and disposition of the spent fuel from the LWR plants. If requested by KEDO, the DPRK shall relinquish any ownership rights over the LWR spent fuel and agree to the transfer of the spent fuel out of its territory as soon as technically possible after the fuel is discharged, through appropriate commercial contracts.

4. Necessary arrangements for the transfer of LWR spent fuel out of the DPRK shall be specified in a separate protocol between KEDO and the DPRK pursuant to the Agreement.

Article IX

Services

1. The DPRK shall process for approval all applications necessary for completion of the LWR project expeditiously and free of charge. These approvals shall include all permits issued by the DPRK nuclear regulatory authority, customs clearance, entry and other permits, licenses, site access rights, and site take-over agreements. In the event that any such approval is delayed beyond the normally required time or denied, the DPRK shall notify KEDO promptly of the reasons therefore, and the schedule and cost for the LWR project may be adjusted as appropriate.

2. KEDO, its contractors and subcontractors, and their respective personnel shall be exempt from DPRK taxes, duties, charges and fees as shall be agreed between KEDO and the DPRK, and expropriation in connection with the LWR project.

3. All personnel sent to the DPRK by KEDO, its contractors and subcontractors shall be allowed unimpeded access to the project site and to appropriate and efficient transportation routes, including air and sea links, to and from the project site as designated by the DPRK and agreed between KEDO and the DPRK. Additional routes will be considers as the progress of the LWR project may require.

4. The DPRK shall, to the extent possible, make available at a fair price port services, transportation, labor, potable water, food, off-site lodging and offices, communications, fuel, electrical power, materials, medical services, currency exchanges and other financial services, and other amenities necessary for living and working by personnel sent to the DPRK by KEDO, its contractors and subcontractors.

5. KEDO, its contractors and subcontractors, and their respective personnel shall be allowed unimpeded use of available means of communications in the DPRK. In addition, KEDO, its contractors and subcontractors shall be permitted by the DPRK to establish secure and independent means of communications for their offices, based on a timely and case-by-case review of equipment requests and in accordance with relevant telecommunications regulations of the DPRK.

6. Details concerning the above-referenced services shall be specified, as appropriate, in one or more separate protocols between KEDO and the DPRK pursuant to the Agreement.

Article X

Nuclear Safety and Regulation

1. KEDO shall be responsible for assuring that design, manufacture, construction, testing, and commissioning of the LWR plants are in compliance with nuclear safety and regulatory codes and standards specified in Article I(3).

2. The DPRK shall issue a site take-over certificate to KEDO upon completion of the site survey. A construction permit shall be issued by the DPRK nuclear regulatory authority to KEDO, prior to the power block excavation, based on its review of the preliminary safety analysis report and the site studies and on its determination of whether the LWR project complies with the nuclear safety and regulatory codes and standards specified in Article I(3). A commissioning permit shall be issued by the DPRK nuclear regulatory authority to KEDO prior to initial fuel loading, based on its review of the final safety analysis report, which includes the as-built design of the LWR plant, and results of non-nuclear commissioning tests. KEDO shall provide the results of nuclear commissioning tests and operator training records to the DPRK in support of its issuance of an operating permit to the operator. KEDO shall provide the DPRK, in a timely manner, with the safety analysis reports, necessary information including that on the codes and standards, and such other documents as KEDO deems necessary in order to make the required determination. The DPRK shall ensure that these permits will be issued in a timely manner not to impede the project schedule.

3. The DPRK shall be responsible for the safe operation and maintenance of the LWR plants, appropriate physical protection, environmental protection, and, consistent with Article VIII(3), the safe storage and disposal of radioactive waste, including spent fuel, in conformity with the set of codes and standards specified in Article I (3). In this regard, the DPRK shall assure that appropriate nuclear regulatory standards and procedures are in place to ensure the safe operation and maintenance of the LWR plants.

4. Prior to the shipment of any fuel assemblies to the DPRK, the DPRK shall observe the provisions set forth in the Convention on Nuclear Safety(done at Vienna, September 20, 1994), the Convention on Early Notification of a Nuclear Accident (adopted at Vienna, September 26, 1986), the Convention on Assistance in the Case of a Nuclear Accident or Radiological Emergency (adopted at Vienna, September 26, 1986), and the Convention on the Physical Protection of Nuclear Material (opened for signature at Vienna and New York, March 3, 1980).

5. After the completion of the LWR plants, KEDO and the DPRK shall conduct safety reviews to ensure the safe operation and maintenance of the LWR plants. In this regard, the DPRK shall provide necessary assistance to enable such reviews to be conducted as expeditiously as possible and shall give due consideration to the results of such reviews. Details concerning the schedule and procedures for conducting the safety reviews shall be specified in a separate protocol between KEDO and the DPRK pursuant to the Agreement.

6. In the event of a nuclear emergency or accident, the DPRK shall permit immediate access to the site and information by personnel sent by KEDO, its contractors and subcontractors to determine the extent of safety concerns and to provide safety assistance.

Article XI

Nuclear Liability

1. The DPRK shall ensure that a legal and financial mechanism is available for meeting claims brought within the DPRK for damages in the event of a nuclear incident(as defined in the Vienna Convention on Civil Liability for Nuclear Damage, done at Vienna, May 21, 1963) in connection with the LWR plants. The legal mechanism shall include the channeling of liability in the event of a nuclear incident to the operator on the basis of absolute liability. The DPRK shall ensure that the operator is able to satisfy such liabilities.

2. Prior to the shipment of any fuel assemblies to the DPRK, the DPRK shall enter into an indemnity agreement with KEDO, and shall secure nuclear liability insurance or other financial security to protect KEDO, its

contractors and subcontractors, and their respective personnel in connection with any third party claims in any court or forum arising from activities undertaken pursuant to the Agreement in the event of nuclear damage or loss occurring inside or outside the territory of the DPRK as a result of a nuclear incident in connection with the LWR plants. Details concerning the indemnity agreement and insurance or other financial security shall be specified in a separate protocol between KEDO and the DPRK pursuant to the Agreement.

3. The DPRK shall bring no claims against KEDO, its contractors and subcontractors, and their respective personnel arising out of any nuclear damage or loss.

4. This Article shall not be construed as acknowledging the jurisdiction of any court or forum or as waiving any immunity of either side.

5. The domestic legal system of the DPRK may provide that, if the operator proves that the nuclear damage resulted wholly or partly either from the gross negligence of the person suffering the damage or from an act or omission of such person done with intent to cause damage, the operation in respect of the damage suffered by such person. The operator shall have a right of recourse only if the damage caused by a nuclear incident results from an act or omission done with intent. For purposes of this paragraph, the terms "person" and "individual" shall have the same meaning as in the Vienna Convention on Civil Liability for Nuclear Damage (done at Vienna, May 21, 1963).

Article XII

Intellectual Property

1. In the course of performing its obligations under the Agreement, each side may receive, directly or indirectly, information relating to the intellectual property of the other side. All such information and any materials or documents containing such information (collectively, the "Intellectual Property") are proprietary and confidential to such other side, whether or not protected by patent or copyright law. Each side agrees to protect the confidentiality of the other side's Intellectual Property and to use it only for the purposes of the LWR project as provided for in the Agreement

and in accordance with international norms, including practices established by the Paris Convention on the Protection of Industrial Property Rights.

2. Except as otherwise agreed between the two sides, neither side shall replicate, copy, or otherwise reproduce any of the equipment or technology of the other side provided in connection with the LWR project.

Article XIII

Assurances

1. The DPRK shall use the reactors, technology, and nuclear material (as defined in accordance with international practice) transferred pursuant to the Agreement, as well as any nuclear material used therein or produced through the use of such items, exclusively for peaceful, non-explosive purposes.

2. The DPRK shall ensure that the reactors, technology, and nuclear material transferred pursuant to the Agreement, as well as any nuclear material used therein or produced through the use of such items, are used properly and exclusively for the purposes of the LWR project.

3. The DPRK shall provide effective physical protection in accordance with international standard with respect to the reactors and nuclear material transferred pursuant to the Agreement, as well as any nuclear material used therein or produced through the use of such items for the useful life of such reactors and nuclear material.

4. The DPRK shall apply IAEA safeguards to the reactors and nuclear material transferred pursuant to the Agreement, as well as any nuclear material used therein or produced through the use of such items, for the useful life of such reactors and nuclear material.

5. The DPRK shall at no time reprocess or increase the enrichment level of any nuclear material transferred pursuant to the Agreement, or any nuclear material used in or produced through the use of any reactor or nuclear material used in or produced through the use of any reactor or nuclear material transferred in the LWR project.

6. The DPRK shall not transfer any nuclear equipment or technology or nuclear material transferred pursuant to the Agreement, or any nuclear material used therein or produced through the use of such items, outside the territory of the DPRK unless otherwise agreed between KEDO and the DPRK, except as provided for in Article VIII(3).

7. The above-referenced assurances may be supplemented by DPRK assurances, through appropriate arrangements, to KEDO members that provide to the DPRK any components controlled under the Export Trigger List of the Nuclear Suppliers Group for the LWR project, if and when such KEDO member of members and the DPRK deem it necessary.

Article XIV

Force Majeure

Either side's performance shall be considered excusably delayed if such delay is due to one or more events that are internationally accepted to constitute force majeure. Each such event is herein referred to as an event of "Force Majeure." The side whose performance is delayed by an event of Force Majeure shall provide notice of such delay to the other side promptly after such event has occurred and shall use such efforts as are reasonable in the circumstances to mitigate such delay and the effect thereof on such side's performance. The two sides shall then consult with each other promptly and in good faith to determine whether alternative performance and the adjustment of the schedule and cost of the LWR project are necessary.

Article XV

Dispute Resolution

1. Any disputes arising out of the interpretation or implementation of the Agreement shall be settled through consultations between KEDO and the DPRK, in conformity with the principles of international law. KEDO and the DPRK shall organize a coordinating committee composed of three people from each side to help settle disputes that may arise in the process of implementing the Agreement.

2. Any dispute that cannot be resolved in this manner shall, at the request of either side and with the consent of the other side, be submitted to an arbitral tribunal composed as follows: KEDO and the DPRK shall each designate one arbitrator, and the two arbitrators so designated shall elect a third, who shall be the Chairman. If, within thirty days of the mutual agreement for arbitration, either KEDO or the DPRK has not designated an arbitrator, either KEDO or the DPRK may request the President of the International Court of Justice to appoint an arbitrator. The same procedure shall apply if, within thirty days of the designation or appointment of the second arbitrator, the third arbitrator has not been elected. A majority of the members of the arbitral tribunal shall constitute a quorum, and all decisions shall require the concurrence of two arbitrators. The arbitral procedure shall be fixed by the tribunal. The decisions of the tribunal shall be binding on KEDO and the DPRK. Each side shall bear the cost of its own arbitrator and its representation in the arbitral proceedings. The cost of the Chairman in discharging his duties and the remaining costs of the arbitral tribunal shall be borne equally by both sides.

Article XVI

Actions in the Event of Noncompliance

1. KEDO and the DPRK shall perform their respective obligations in good faith to achieve the basic objectives of the Agreement.

2. In the event that either side fails to take its respective steps specified in the Agreement, the other side shall have the right to require the immediate payment of any amounts due and financial losses in connection with the LWR project.

3. In the event of late payment or nonpayment by either side with respect to financial obligations to the other side incurred in implementing the Agreement, the other side shall have the right to assess and apply penalties against that side. Details concerning the assessment and application of such penalties shall be specified in a separate protocol between KEDO and the DPRK pursuant to the Agreement.

Article XVII

Amendments

1. The Agreement may be amended by written agreement between the two sides.

2. Any amendment shall enter into force on the date of its signature.

Article XVIII

Entry into Force

1. The Agreement shall constitute an international agreement between KEDO and the DPRK, and shall be binding on both sides under international law.

2. The Agreement shall enter into force on the date of its signature.

3. The Annexes to Agreement shall be an integral part of the Agreement.

4. The Protocols pursuant to the Agreement shall enter into force on the date of their respective signature.

IN WITNESS WHEREOF, the undersigned, being duly authorized, have signed the Agreement.

DONE at New York City on this 15th day of December, 1995, in duplicate in the English language.

Joint Statement of the Six Party Talks, September 19, 2005

For the cause of peace and stability on the Korean Peninsula and in northeast Asia at large, the six parties held in a spirit of mutual respect and equality serious and practical talks concerning the denuclearization of the Korean Peninsula on the basis of the common understanding of the previous three rounds of talks and agreed in this context to the following:

1) The six parties unanimously reaffirmed that the goal of the six-party talks is the verifiable denuclearization of the Korean Peninsula in a peaceful manner.

   The Democratic People's Republic of Korea (North Korea) committed to abandoning all nuclear weapons and existing nuclear programs and returning at an early date to the treaty on the nonproliferation of nuclear weapons (NPT) and to IAEA (International Atomic Energy Agency) safeguards.
   The United States affirmed that is has no nuclear weapons on the Korean Peninsula and has no intention to attack or invade the DPRK with nuclear or conventional weapons.
   The ROK (South Korea) reaffirmed its commitment not to receive or deploy nuclear weapons in accordance with the 1992 joint declaration of the Denuclearization of the Korean Peninsula, while affirming that there exist no nuclear weapons within its territory.
   The 1992 joint declaration of the Denuclearization of the Korean Peninsula should be observed and implemented.
   The DPRK stated that it has the right to peaceful uses of nuclear energy.
   The other parties expressed their respect and agreed to discuss at an appropriate time the subject of the provision of light-water reactor to the DPRK.

2) The six parties undertook, in their relations, to abide by the purposes and principles of the Charter of the United Nations and

recognized norms of international relations.

The DPRK and the United States undertook to respect each other's sovereignty, exist peacefully together and take steps to normalize their relations subject to their respective bilateral policies.

The DPRK and Japan undertook to take steps to normalize their relations in accordance with the (2002) Pyongyang Declaration, on the basis of the settlement of unfortunate past and the outstanding issues of concern.

3) The six parties undertook to promote economic cooperation in the fields of energy, trade and investment, bilaterally and/or multilaterally.

China, Japan, the Republic of Korea (ROK), Russia and the U.S. stated their willingness to provide energy assistance to the DPRK. The ROK reaffirmed its proposal of July 12, 2005, concerning the provision of 2 million kilowatts of electric power to the DPRK.

4) Committed to joint efforts for lasting peace and stability in northeast Asia. The directly related parties will negotiate a permanent peace regime on the Korean Peninsula at an appropriate separate forum.

The six parties agreed to explore ways and means for promoting security cooperation in northeast Asia.

5) The six parties agreed to take coordinated steps to implement the aforementioned consensus in a phased manner in line with the principle of "commitment for commitment, action for action."

6) The six parties agreed to hold the fifth round of the six party talks in Beijing in early November 2005 at a date to be determined through consultations.

References

Bang, Kiyol. *South and North Korean Energy Demand and Supply.* Gyonggido: Korea Energy Economics Institute, 1999.

Jung, Woojin. *North Korean Energy Industry.* Seoul: Korean Overseas Information Service, 1996.

Kim, Kyungsul. *North Korean Energy Problems.* Gyonggido: Korea Energy Economics Institute, 2003.

Korea National Statistical Office. *Comparison of South and North Korean Socio-Economic Data.* Seoul: Korea National Statistical Office, 2004.

Minitry of Unification. *Gaeseong Idustrial Complex Guide.* Seoul: Ministry of Unification (Office of Gaeseong Industrial Complex Project), 2005.

North Korea Economics Forum. *North Korean Energy.* Seoul: Korea Gas Corporation R&D Division, 1997.

Paik, Hoon. A *Study on Harmonization between Multilateral and Bilateral Energy Cooperation in Northeast Asia.* New Asia Economy and Technology Federation, 2004.

Chanlett-Avery, Emma. "Rising Energy Competition and Energy Security in Northeast Asia: Issues for U.S. Policy." *CRS Report for Congress.* Washington, D.C.: Congressional Research Service, July 14, 2004.

Chung, Youngrong. "The Utilization of Factor Endowment." *Economy Research.* Vol. 2. Pyongyang, 2001.

Jung, Woojin. "Comparison between South and North Korean Energy Systems." *Petroleum Association Magazine.* 1993.

Kim, Dukho. "Necessary Requirements of Military First Era." *Economy Research.* Vol. 2. Pyongyang, 2004.

Kim, Jinwoo. "Energy Security of Northeast Asia: Current State,

Energy Demand/Supply Projection and Investment Needs." Paper prepared for the KEEI-IEA Joint Conference on *Energy Challenges in Northeast Asia and Project Proposals in 2004*. Seoul: KEEI-IEA, 2004.

Ministry of Unification. "Small and Medium Size Power Plants of North Korea." Seoul: Ministry of Unification, June 21, 2004.

_____. "Energy Provision to North Korea." Seoul: Ministry of Unification, September 22, 2005.

Niksch, Larry A. "North Korea's Nuclear Weapons Program." *CRS Issue Brief for Congress*. Washington, D.C.: Congressional Research Service, August 31, 2005.

Valencia, Mark J. and James P. Doran. "Multilateral Cooperation in Northeast Asia's Energy Sector: Possibilities and Problems." *Energy and Security in Northeast Asia: Supply and Demand, Conflict and Cooperation*. Institute on Global Conflict and Cooperation, February 1998. <http://www.ciaonet.org/wps/shs01/igcc36ac.html>

Von Hippel, David and Peter Hayes. "The DPRK Energy Sector: Recent Status, Problems, Cooperation Opportunities, and Constraints." Prepared for the Workshop on *Future Multilateral Economic Cooperation with the Democratic People's Republic of Korea*, Stanley Foundation, June 15~17, 2005.

_____. "DPRK Energy Sector: Current Status and Scenarios for 2000 and 2005." Paper prepared for the conference. *Economic Integration of the Korean Peninsula*. September 5~6, 1997.

Bank of Korea Data: <http://www.bok.or.kr/template/main/html/index.jsp?tbl=tbl_FM0000000066_CA0000000701>.

Korea Trade-Investment Promotion Agency Data: <http://www.globalwindow.org/front/nk04/nk04_view.jsp?seq No=933>.